Grade One

Music Theory

2nd Edition

(ABRSM 2018 Syllabus)

GRADE ONE MUSIC THEORY COURSE AND EXERCISES

By Victoria Williams

www.mymusictheory.com

2nd Edition

ISBN-13: 978-1530018574

ISBN-10: 1530018579

CONTENTS

INTRODUCTION

This book was written for students who are preparing to take the ABRSM Grade One Music Theory exam. Parents of younger students will also find it helpful, as well as busy music teachers who are trying to fit a lot of music theory teaching into a very short time during instrumental lessons.

This updated 2nd edition has been revised to reflect minor changes to the ABRSM syllabus effective from 1st January 2018.

Each topic is broken down into digestible steps, and for best results the lessons should be followed in the order they are presented, as the acquired knowledge is cumulative.

After each topic, you will find a page or so of practice exercises, to help you consolidate what you have learned. Answers are provided on the page following the exercises.

At the end of the book there is a practice test which is in a similar style to the actual exam papers.

Further tests for Grade One candidates are also available in "30 Grade One Tests" by the same author. These comprise a set of twenty topic-based tests, and ten score-based revision tests.

I also highly recommend purchasing ABRSM past papers before sitting an actual exam. These can be obtained from shop.abrsm.org, Amazon or your local sheet music reseller.

You are welcome to photocopy the pages of this book for your own use, or to use with your pupils if you are a music teacher.

ABOUT THE AUTHOR

Victoria Williams graduated with a BA Hons degree in Music from the University of Leeds, UK, in 1995, where she specialised in notation and musicology. She also holds the AmusTCL Diploma in Music Theory from Trinity College London, with distinction.

In 2007 she created the website www.mymusictheory.com, which initially offered free lessons for Grade 5 ABRSM Music Theory candidates. Over the years, the full spectrum of ABRSM theory grades has been added, making MyMusicTheory one of the only websites worldwide offering a comprehensive, free, music theory training programme aligned with the ABRSM syllabuses.

You can connect with Victoria Williams in the following ways:

www.mymusictheory.com

info@mymusictheory.com

www.facebook.com/mymusictheory

www.twitter.com/mymusictheory

https://www.youtube.com/user/musictheoryexpert

1. THE STAFF AND NOTES

STAFF NOTATION IN MUSIC

Music is written down in a number of different ways around the world. In the West, most instruments use a method called **staff notation**.

The music staff, or stave, is made up of 5 horizontal lines: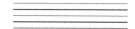

On the music staff, notes are placed on the lines:

and in the spaces:

The **pitch** of a note (how high or low-sounding it is) depends on which line or space it's written on.

The **time length** of a note depends on the colour and shape of the note. Notes can have black or white heads, and some have stems (sticks) attached.

In this lesson we will learn about **pitch**. We'll look at the time length of notes in lesson 4.

THE TREBLE CLEF

We always put a **clef** at the beginning of the music staff. A clef is just a symbol which identifies **one** note by name. We can work out all the other notes from this one.

The most commonly used clef is the **treble clef**, which looks like this:

The treble clef tells us where on the music staff we should write the note G.

We draw the treble clef so that the **curly** bit in the middle forms a sort of **circle** around the second line on the staff- a note written on this line is a G. Sometimes the treble clef is called the "**G** clef" because of this.

The treble clef is used for music which is quite high-pitched. Instruments which use this clef include the flute, clarinet, violin and trumpet. It is also used for female voices, and the right hand of piano music.

Now we know where the note G is, we can work out all the other notes on the staff.

LETTER NAMES

We use the letter names A-G (always written in **capital** letters) to identify notes.

After G, the next note is A, (because we start the sequence again).

G is on a line on the treble clef music staff, so the next note up, A, is in a space:

The next note up is B, which is on a line:

Here are all the lines and spaces of the music staff filled up:

You can try to remember the letter names of the notes on lines by learning

Every **G**ood **B**oy **D**eserves **F**ootball

And you can learn the notes in the spaces by memorising

D – FACE – G

Or you can make up your own silly sentences to help you remember!

The note which comes before the first D in this series is called **middle C**.

On a piano keyboard, it's the C nearest the keyhole.

Middle C is written under the stave, with a short line through the note - you can think of this line as an extension of the stave. The short line is called a **ledger line**.

1. THE STAFF AND NOTES EXERCISES

1. Give the letter names of the notes marked with a star.

2. What is the name of the clef used in this melody?

3. Give the letter name of the highest note.

4. Give the letter name of the lowest note.

5. Draw a circle around "middle C".

6. How many F's are there?

7. Starting from D and going **upwards**, write the letter names of the notes found in the **spaces** in this clef.

8. Now starting on F and going **downwards**, write the letter names of the notes found on the **lines**.

9. Draw a treble clef:

10. Using this shape of note ○ , write the notes as described below:

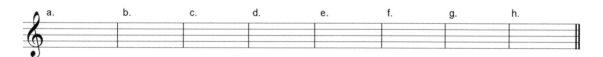

a. G on a line	b. D in a space	c. C in a space	d. E in space
e. C on a ledger line	f. F in a space	g. B on a line	h. F on a line

1. THE STAFF AND NOTES ANSWERS

1.

2. Treble clef.

3. G.

4. C.

5.

6. 3

7. D – F – A – C – E

8. F – D – B – G – E – (middle C)

9.

10.

2. BASS CLEF

We have already learned about our first clef, the treble clef.

For most low-pitched music, (where most of it is lower than middle C), we use the **bass clef**. The bass clef is used by many low-pitched instruments, such as the tuba, bassoon, and double bass. It's also the normal clef for the left hand in piano music, and the bass voice.

The bass clef looks like this:

The two dots on the right hand side of the bass clef are placed either side of the line where we can find the note **F**, so it's also known as the **F clef**.

This is the first F below middle C.

Note Names

We can work out the other notes just like we did with the treble clef. Here are the notes on the lines:

And here are the notes in the spaces:

The note above B on the top of the staff is **middle C**. It's useful to be able to write middle C in both clefs. We use a ledger line (small line which makes an extra line on the staff) for it to sit on, just like we did in the treble clef (but in the bass clef it is above the staff):

Remember that in the treble clef, middle C is below the stave:

2. BASS CLEF EXERCISES

1. Give the letter names of the notes marked with a star.

2. Draw a circle around "middle C" in the above melody.

3. How many Gs are there in the melody?

4. What is the note on the middle line of the bass clef?

5. The two dots on the bass clef are either side of the line which shows which note?

6. Draw the correct clefs (treble or bass). The first one has been done for you.

7. Using this shape of note **O** , write the notes as described below:

   a. C in a space
   b. F on a line
   c. G on a line
   d. B in a space
   e. Middle C
   f. E in a space
   g. A in a space
   h. D on a line

2. BASS CLEF ANSWERS

1.

2.

3. Three

4. D

5. F

6.

7.

3. ACCIDENTALS

In music theory, the word "accidentals" is used to describe some notes which have been slightly altered. Accidentals are symbols which are written immediately **before** the note on the stave - they can be "sharps", "flats" or "naturals". In this unit we'll have a look at what accidentals are exactly and how they are used in music theory.

THE OCTAVE

To begin, let's look at a piano keyboard.

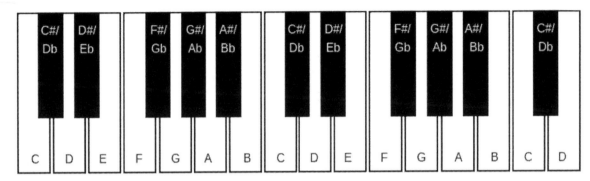

How many different notes are there between two Cs (don't count the C's twice)?

If we count all the **black and white** notes, we'll find there are 12 different notes. This span of notes is called an "octave". This isn't only true for the piano – every instrument uses the same series of notes.

SHARPS AND FLATS

We have 12 different notes, but we only use 7 letters of the alphabet. We use the words "sharp" (=higher) and "flat" (=lower) with a letter name, to cover all those "in-between" notes. Sharps and flats are two kinds of "accidentals". We can use symbols for accidentals, instead of the words sharp and flat.

♯ Sharp symbol

♭ Flat symbol

Find the notes C and D on the keyboard (they are both white notes). In between them, you'll see a black note. We can say that this note is a bit higher than C, so it is "C sharp" (C#), or we can say it is a bit lower than D, so it is also "D flat" (Db).

NATURALS

The third type of accidental we are going to look at is called the "natural". We use the word "natural" (or the symbol ♮) to say that a note is neither sharp nor flat. This is very useful, because sometimes when a note has already been altered by an accidental (flat or sharp), we need to put a natural sign in to tell the player that it isn't flat or sharp any more.

Flats, sharps and naturals make up the main accidentals, and they are the only accidentals you need to know for grade one music theory.

Questions on Accidentals

In the ABRSM Grade 1 music theory exam, you are sometimes asked to identify the higher or lower note of a pair. The notes will be in the same position on the staff, but have different accidentals next to them.

Remember that flats are **low** and sharps are **high**, while naturals are in the **middle**.

Which of these two notes is lower?

 The first note is G natural, and the second note is G flat. Flats are lower, so the second note is lower.

Which of these two notes is lower?

 The first note is G natural, and the second note is G sharp. Sharps are higher, so the first note is lower.

Notice that we write the accidental symbol on the same **line or space** of the note it changes.

Bar lines and Accidentals

When an accidental has been written, all the other notes which are the same pitch, (or position on the staff), are also affected by the accidental, but **only until a bar line is drawn**.

Here's an example:

Note 1 is natural, because we haven't put any accidentals.

Note 2 is flattened by the flat symbol.

Note 3 is also flattened by the symbol from number 2, because it's in the same bar.

Note 4 is natural, because the bar line cancels the effect of the flat.

Note 5 is flattened by the accidental symbol.

Note 6 is naturalised by the bar line.

Notes of the same letter name, but which occupy different positions on the staff, are **not** affected by each other's accidentals.

 Note 3 is a G natural. The flat on number 2 doesn't affect it, because it's not the same pitch – it's an octave higher.

3. ACCIDENTALS EXERCISES

1. Give the letter names of these notes. Use the correct symbol for sharps and flats.

2. Complete the sentence. "Accidentals affect all the next notes written on the same line/space until a

_____ is drawn."

3. Give the letter name of the notes marked with a star. Include the ♯ or ♭ sign when needed.

4. Circle all the F sharps in this melody.

5. Circle the **higher** or **lower** note, as indicated.

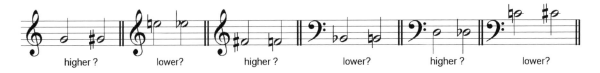

higher ?   lower?   higher ?   lower?   higher ?   lower?

3. ACCIDENTALS ANSWERS

1.

C#   Eb   D#   G#   Ab   F#   Bb

2. Bar line.

3.

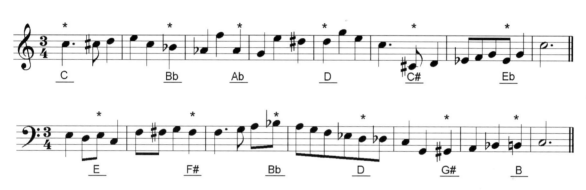

C   Bb   Ab   D   C#   Eb

E   F#   Bb   D   G#   B

4.

5.

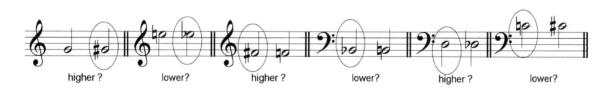

higher ?   lower?   higher ?   lower?   higher ?   lower?

4. TIME NAMES OF NOTES

This page contains the UK note names. USA note names can be found on the next page.

Music is played to a regular beat, which you can count. You can count fast or slow, but you must keep a **steady** beat going, for example, count once per second.

NOTE SHAPES

The longest note used in most music is the **semibreve**. Shape: white oval. Count: 1-2-3-4.

Half a semibreve is a **minim**. Shape: white oval with a stem (stick). Count 1-2.

Half a minim is a **crotchet**. Shape: black oval with a stem. Count 1.

Half a crotchet is a **quaver**. Shape: black oval with a stem and a tail. Count ½.

Half a quaver is a **semiquaver**. Shape: black oval with a stem and two tails. Count ¼.

BEAMED NOTES

Quavers and semiquavers can be joined together. This is done to make them easier to read, and to help show where the complete beats in the bar are. Here are two bars with the same notes. The first bar contains the unbeamed notes, and in the second they are beamed together.

To make a beam, remove the tail(s) and replace with a straight line(s), joined to the next quaver/semiquaver. Note with two tails need two beams.

unbeamed   beamed

HOW LONG IS A CROTCHET?

Notes don't have a length fixed in seconds – their actual length can change from piece to piece.

- In one piece a crotchet may last about a second, which means a minim=2 seconds and a quaver= ½ second.

- In another piece a crotchet may only last ½ a second, making a minim=1 second and a quaver= ¼ second.

Usually a crotchet lasts between ½ and 1 second; the **tempo** instructions of a piece will guide you.

Music is played to a regular beat, which you can count. You can count fast or slow, but you must keep a **steady** beat going, for example, count once per second.

NOTE SHAPES

To show how long a note should be held for, we use different note shapes.

The longest note used in most music is the **whole note**. Shape: white oval. Count 1-2-3-4.

Half a whole note is a **half note**. Shape: white oval with a stem (stick). Count 1-2.

Half a half note is a **quarter note**. Shape: black oval with a stem. Count 1.

Half a quarter note is an eighth note. Shape: black oval with a stem and a tail. Count ½.

Half an eighth note is a **sixteenth note**. Shape: black oval with a stem and two tails. Count ¼.

BEAMED NOTES

Eighths and sixteenths can be joined together. This is done to make them easier to read, and to help show where the beats in the measure lie. Here are two measures with the same notes. The first measure contains the unbeamed notes, and in the second they are beamed together.

To make a beam, remove the tail(s) and replace with a straight line(s), joined to the next eighth/sixteenth. Notes with two tails will need two beams.

unbeamed   beamed

HOW LONG IS A QUARTER NOTE?

Notes don't have a length fixed in seconds – their actual length can change from piece to piece.

- In one piece a quarter note may last about a second, which means a half note=2 seconds and an eighth note = ½ second.

- In another piece a quarter note may only last ½ a second, making a half note =1 second and an eighth note = ¼ second.

Usually a quarter note lasts between ½ and 1 second; the **tempo** instructions of a piece will guide you.

WRITING NOTES

1. Don't write note heads **too big**.

2. Notes on a line must not **touch** the next line above or below.

This note is badly written - the top of the note head touches the next line:

This is how it should look:

3. Notes in space must not **cross over** the line above or below.

This badly written note crosses the line below it:

This is how it should look:

3. Stems can point up or down: if the note is above the middle line, it should point down (and vice versa). Notes ON the middle line can have their stems in either direction.

4. Accidentals go on the **left** side of the note. Write them carefully on the same line/space as the note, and don't write them too big!

Here is a badly written sharp – the sign is too large, and crosses the "D" line instead of being in the "C" space.

This is how it should look:

4. TIME NAMES OF NOTES EXERCISES (UK)

1. Match the notes with their time names.

Semibreve	Minim	Crotchet	Quaver	Semiquaver
♪	♩	𝅝	𝅗𝅥	♪

2. Answer the questions. The first one has been done for you as an example.

   a. How many semiquavers is a quaver worth? ____2____

   b. How many quavers is a minim worth? _____

   c. How many minims is a crotchet worth? _____

   d. How many semiquavers is a crotchet worth? _____

   e. How many quavers is a semibreve worth? _____

3. Copy this melody as neatly as you can.

4. Find and circle 4 notation errors in this melody. Rewrite it correctly.

4. TIME NAMES OF NOTES EXERCISES (USA)

1. Match the notes with their time names.

Whole note	Half note	Quarter note	Eighth note	Sixteenth note
♪ (eighth)	♩ (quarter)	𝅝 (whole)	𝅗𝅥 (half)	♪ (sixteenth)

2. Answer the questions. The first one has been done for you as an example.

   a. How many sixteenths is an eighth worth? ____2____

   b. How many eighths is a half note worth? _____

   c. How many half notes is a quarter note worth? _____

   d. How many sixteenths is a quarter note worth? _____

   e. How many eighths is a whole note worth? _____

3. Copy this melody as neatly as you can.

4. Find and circle 4 notation errors in this melody. Rewrite it correctly.

22

4. TIME NAMES OF NOTES ANSWERS

1.

	○	𝅗𝅥	♩	♪	𝅘𝅥𝅯
UK names	Semibreve	Minim	Crotchet	Quaver	Semiquaver
USA names	Whole note	Half note	Quarter note	8th note	16th note

2.

b. 4

c. ½

d. 4

e. 8

3.

Compare your answer with the original.

4.

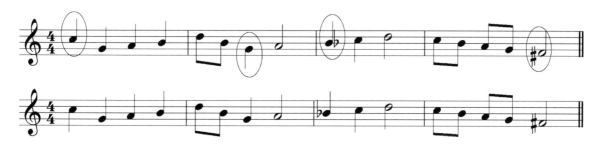

5. TIME NAMES OF RESTS (UK)

A rest symbol means silence. Each of the time values for notes which you learnt in lesson 4 has an equivalent rest symbol.

Semiquaver   Quaver   Crotchet   Minim   Semibreve

If you find the crotchet rest difficult to draw, you can draw it as a backwards quaver rest instead:

The minim and semibreve rests are both black rectangles, but

- the minim rest **sits** on the middle line
- the semibreve rest **hangs** from the 2nd line.

The semibreve rest is sometimes used as a **whole bar rest**.

If so, it is written in the **centre** of the bar, and its time value is however many beats are needed in that melody.

For example, each bar in this melody adds up to three crotchet beats. The whole bar rest is used for one full bar. In this case, the rest represents three crotchet beats (not four).

5. TIME NAMES OF RESTS (USA)

A rest symbol means silence. Each of the time values for notes which you learnt in lesson 4 has an equivalent rest symbol.

If you find the quarter rest difficult to draw, you can draw it as a backwards eighth rest instead:

The half and whole rests are both black rectangles, but

- the half rest **sits** on the middle line
- the whole rest **hangs** from the 2nd line.

The whole rest is sometimes used as a **whole measure rest**.

If so, it is written in the **centre** of the measure, and its time value is however many beats are needed in that melody.

For example, each bar in this melody adds up to three quarter note beats. The whole measure rest is used for one full measure. In this case, the rest represents three quarter note beats (not four).

5. TIME NAMES OF RESTS EXERCISES

1. Practice drawing each of the rest shapes on the empty stave below.

2. Write the rest which has the same time value, for each of these notes.

3. Write out the 5 rests from question 1 in order, from **longest to shortest**, and label them with their names.

4. Write a whole bar rest in the second bar.

5. How can you tell the difference between a minim (half) and semibreve (whole) rest?

_____

5. TIME NAMES OF RESTS ANSWERS

1. Compare your answers with the originals.

2.

3.

(UK) Semibreve   Minim   Crotchet   Quaver   Semiquaver   (USA) Whole   Half   Quarter   Eighth   Sixteenth

4.

5. The minim (half) rest **sits on the middle line**, the semibreve (whole) **hangs from the 2nd line.**

6. DOTTED NOTES AND RESTS (UK)

A dot on the right hand side of a note **increases its length by 50%**. Or in other words, it is the same as 1 ½ times that note length. Add **the note** to **half of itself**, to find its length.

For example, if you put a dot on a crotchet, it is worth one crotchet plus half a crotchet, or 1.5 crotchets:

If you put a dot on a minim, it is worth one minim plus half a minim, or 1.5 minims:

A minim is worth two crotchets, so a dotted minim is worth 3 crotchets (2 + half of 2):

Rests can also be dotted.

Here is a dotted crotchet rest. It has the same value as 1.5 crotchet rests.

6. DOTTED NOTES AND RESTS (USA)

A dot on the right hand side of a note **increases its length by 50%**. Or in other words, it is the same as 1 ½ times that note length. Add **the note** to **half of itself**, to find its length.

For example, if you put a dot on a quarter note, it is worth one quarter note plus half a quarter note, or 1.5 quarter notes:

If you put a dot on a half note, it is worth one half note plus half a half note, or 1.5 half notes:

A half notes is worth two quarter notes, so a dotted half note is worth 3 quarter notes (2 + half of 2):

Rests can also be dotted.

Here is a dotted quarter rest. It has the same value as 1.5 quarter rests.

6. DOTTED NOTES AND RESTS EXERCISES (UK)

1. Explain how a dot affects the time value of a note.

2. Copy out these notes in order of time value, from longest to shortest.

3. Write ONE note which is worth the same as the notes added together. An example is given.

4. How many **quavers** are there in a **dotted crotchet**? _____

5. How many **crotchets** are there in a **dotted minim**? _____

6. How many **dotted crotchets** are there in a **dotted minim**? _____

7. How many **semiquavers** are there in a **dotted crotchet**? _____

6. DOTTED NOTES AND RESTS EXERCISES (USA)

1. Explain how a dot affects the time value of a note.

2. Copy out these notes in order of time value, from longest to shortest.

3. Write ONE note which is worth the same as the notes added together. An example is given.

4. How many **eighth notes** are there in a **dotted quarter note**? _____

5. How many **quarter notes** are there in a **dotted half note**? _____

6. How many **dotted quarter notes** are there in a **dotted half note**? _____

7. How many **sixteenth notes** are there in a **dotted quarter note**? _____

6. DOTTED NOTES AND RESTS ANSWERS

1. A dot increases the time value of the note by 50%.

2.

3.

4. 3

5. 3

6. 2

7. 6

7. TIME SIGNATURES (UK)

A time signature is a symbol which we write at the beginning of a piece of music to show how many **beats** there are in one **bar**.

Time signatures are made of two numbers, one on top of the other.

Here's a time signature:

$$\frac{2}{4}$$

Time signatures are written after the clef and key signature, and only appear at the beginning of a piece of music, not on every stave.

GRADE ONE REQUIREMENTS

In Grade 1 music theory you need to know three time signatures: 2/4, 3/4 and 4/4. (Note that the line used here to separate the numbers is not actually used on the stave).

THE BOTTOM NUMBER

The bottom number in a time signature tells you the **type** of beat we need to count in each bar.

The number 4 represents a crotchet beat. So, in Grade One music theory we only need to think about counting crotchets, because the lower number is "4" in all three time signatures you need to know at this grade.

THE TOP NUMBER

The top number tells us **how many** beats we need to count in each complete bar.

So,

$\frac{2}{4}$ means we should count two crotchet beats in each complete bar

$\frac{3}{4}$ means we should count three crotchet beats, and

$\frac{4}{4}$ means we should count four crotchet beats.

Bar Lines

We draw vertical bar lines through the stave to divide the music up into complete bars.

(Sometimes the first and last bars of a piece can be incomplete, but all the bars in between must be complete ones).

Here's an example in 2/4:

The values of the notes in each bar always add up to two crotchet beats.

Here's an example in 3/4. This time the first bar is incomplete:

The values of the notes in each bar add up to three crotchets, except in the first and last bars which are incomplete.

Working out the Time Signature

In the Grade 1 music theory exam, you might have to work out the time signature of a short piece.

Don't forget that in the Grade One music theory exam, you only need to know 2/4, 3/4 and 4/4, so the right answer must be one of these three time signatures.

To work out the time signature, add up the note values in one bar, counting a crotchet as 1.

Remember that a quaver = ½ a crotchet, a semiquaver = ¼, a minim=2 crotchets and a semibreve = 4. Also, don't forget that a dot increases the length of a note by half of its value.

When you are practising, write them out, like this:

Count up the notes in each bar, and work out how many crotchets each bar is worth.

Bar 1 is worth four crotchets (and so are all the others). Four crotchets per bar means the time signature is 4/4.

Here's another example:

There are 2 crotchet beats per bar, so this is 2/4 time.

ADDING MISSING BAR LINES

In your music theory exam, you might have to add the missing bar lines to a short tune with a given time signature.

Let's work out where to put the bar lines in the following melody. Use the same method: count the crotchet beats. The first bar line has been given.

First, look at the time signature. How many beats do you need to count? (Don't forget, the top number on the time signature tells us how many to count.)

In this melody, the time signature is 3/4, so we need to count **three** crotchets in every bar.

It's a good idea to pencil the note values in as you do this exercise - it's easier to work out where you've made a mistake and to double check your answers if you've done so. Let's pencil in those note values:

Start by grouping together fractions to make up complete beats.

Then add the beats together, until you reach the number you need - remember it will always be 2, 3 or 4 crotchets in the Grade One music theory exam.

Then draw a bar line, (use a ruler for neatness).

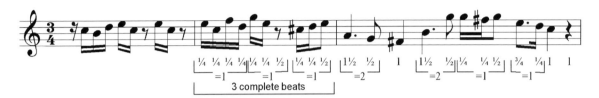

After each bar line you draw, start counting again. Repeat the process until you get to the end of the melody.

Your last bar should also have the full number of beats (in the Grade One music theory exam that is, but not always in real life!) Double check your answer - go back and count each bar again.

If one of your bars has a different number of beats to the others, you have made a mistake!

Make sure that your bar lines are totally vertical (not leaning to one side or the other), that they don't poke up higher or lower than the staff, and that they are placed about one note-head's width away from the note on the right.

Look at the first bar line that you were given as an example, and use it as a guideline.

7. TIME SIGNATURES (USA)

A time signature is a symbol which we write at the beginning of a piece of music to show how many beats there are in one measure.

Time signatures are made of two numbers, one on top of the other.

Here's a time signature:

$$\frac{2}{4}$$

Time signatures are written after the clef and key signature, and only appear at the beginning of a piece of music, not on every staff.

GRADE ONE REQUIREMENTS

In Grade 1 music theory you need to know three time signatures: 2/4, 3/4 and 4/4. (Note that the line used here to separate the numbers is not used on the staff).

THE BOTTOM NUMBER

The bottom number in a time signature tells you the **type** of beat we need to count in each measure.

The number 4 represents a quarter note beat. So, in Grade One music theory we only need to think about counting quarter notes, because the lower number is "4" in all three time signatures you need to know at this grade.

THE TOP NUMBER

The top number tells us **how many** beats we need to count in each complete measure.

So,

$\frac{2}{4}$ means we should count two quarter note beats in each complete measure

$\frac{3}{4}$ means we should count three quarter note beats, and

$\frac{4}{4}$ means we should count four quarter note beats.

BAR LINES

We draw vertical bar lines through the staff to divide the music up into complete measures.

(Sometimes the first and last measures of a piece can be incomplete, but all the measures in between must be complete ones).

Here's an example in 2/4:

The values of the notes in each measure always add up to two quarter note beats.

Here's an example in 3/4. This time the first measure is incomplete:

The values of the notes in each measure add up to three quarter notes, except in the first and last measures which are incomplete.

WORKING OUT THE TIME SIGNATURE

In the Grade 1 music theory exam, you might have to work out the time signature of a short piece.

Don't forget that in the Grade One music theory exam, you only need to know 2/4, 3/4 and 4/4, so the right answer must be one of these three.

To work out the time signature, add up the note values in one measure, counting a quarter note as 1.

Remember that an eighth note = ½ a quarter note, a sixteenth note = ¼, a half note=2 quarter notes and a whole note = 4. Also, don't forget that a dot increases the length of a note by half of its value.

When you are practicing, write them out, like this:

Count up the notes in each measure, and work out how many quarter notes each measure is worth.

Measure 1 is worth four quarter notes (and so are all the others). Four quarter notes per measure means the time signature is 4/4.

Here's another example:

There are 2 quarter note beats per measure, so this is 2/4 time.

ADDING MISSING BAR LINES

In your music theory exam, you might have to add the missing bar lines to a short tune with a given time signature.

Let's work out where to put the bar lines in the following melody. Use the same method: count the quarter note beats. The first bar line has been given.

First, look at the time signature. How many beats do you need to count? (Don't forget, the top number on the time signature tells us how many to count.)

In this melody, the time signature is 3/4, so we need to count **three** quarter notes in every measure.

It's a good idea to pencil the note values in as you do this exercise - it's easier to work out where you've made a mistake and to double check your answers if you've done so. Let's pencil in those note values:

Start by grouping together fractions to make up complete beats.

Then add the beats together, until you reach the number you need - remember it will always be 2, 3 or 4 quarter notes in the Grade One music theory exam.

Then draw a bar line, (use a ruler for neatness).

After each bar line you draw, start counting again. Repeat the process until you get to the end of the melody.

Your last measure should also have the full number of beats (in the Grade One music theory exam that is, but not always in real life!) Double check your answer - go back and count each measure again.

If one of your measures has a different number of beats to the others, you have made a mistake!

Make sure that your bar lines are totally vertical (not leaning to one side or the other), that they don't poke up higher or lower than the staff, and that they are placed about one note-head's width away from the note on the right.

Look at the first bar line that you were given as an example, and use it as a guideline.

7. TIME SIGNATURES EXERCISES
EXERCISE 1

    a.   What does the "3" in the time signature of 3/4 mean?

    b.   Which time signature is used for four crotchet (quarter note) beats per bar?

    c.   What does the lower number in a time signature refer to?

    d.   To work out if a melody is in 2/4, 3/4 or 4/4 time, you need to count the number of

    _____ per bar.

EXERCISE 2

In this melody, the time signature changes **every bar**. Write the correct time signature at the start of **each bar**.

EXERCISE 3

Add bar lines to the following melodies:

a.

b.

c.

7. TIME SIGNATURES ANSWERS

Exercise 1

    a.   Count three beats per bar.

    b.   4/4

    c.   The type of beats you should count.

    d.   Crotchets (quarter notes).

Exercise 2

Exercise 3

a.

b.

c.

8. BEAMING (UK)

Notes which are smaller than a crotchet - quavers and semiquavers – have curved tails attached to their stems.

To make music easier to read, we normally group these small notes together in **complete beats**. To do this, we join the tails together, making them into a straight line.

We call this line a "beam"- they are **beamed notes**.

MAKING BEAMED NOTES

Notes with one tail (quavers and dotted quavers) have one beam. Semiquavers have two tails so they have two beams, which are drawn quite close together.

Here are some examples of beamed quaver notes.

Quavers can be beamed to semiquavers like this:

We can also join dotted quavers to semiquavers with beams, like this:

Notice that the lower semiquaver beam is quite short. This is a cut-off beam.

Cut-off beams should be about as wide as the note-head. They can point in either direction, depending on which side of the quaver they are on. They will often point **towards** a dotted note.

Here's a different example of beamed notes which have cut-off beams:

BEAMING AND BEATS

In the time signatures you need to know for Grade 1 Music Theory (2/4, 3/4 and 4/4), the **beat** is always represented by a **crotchet** time value.

(In other time signatures the beat could be a quaver or minim. However, in this lesson we are assuming the beat is always a crotchet.)

In each bar, some notes are played a tiny bit louder than others - this slight accent is what gives music its feeling of pulse.

Beats are categorised as follows:

- **Strong beat**: this is the strongest accent in the bar and falls right at the beginning of the bar.

- **Weak beat**: these are the other crotchet beats of the bar.

- **Off beat**: these are any notes which fall in between the strong and/or weak beats.

The rules for correct beaming depend on the **time signature** of the music.

You'll need to learn the rules for each time signature separately, as well as these general rules:

- The quavers and semiquavers should be joined together to make the crotchet beat **easy to see**.

- Beams never cross over the bar lines.

- The first note of a beamed group must never fall **on an off beat**, unless it's preceded by a rest or a dotted note.

BEAMING AND RESTS

We can include rests inside a group of beamed notes. Rests themselves are never beamed - we simply squeeze them between the notes.

We can change their vertical position on the stave if we need to, to make the music clearer.

The semiquaver rest has been moved downwards a little bit, so that it doesn't get mixed up with the beam lines.

Beaming in 2/4 Time

In 2/4 time there are two crotchet beats per bar. There is one **strong beat**, which is the first beat of the bar. The second crotchet beat is the weak beat.

Notes are normally beamed together to make up one crotchet beat. Here are some examples.

If there are four quavers in a bar, they can all be beamed together.

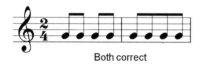

Both correct

Beaming in 3/4 Time

In 3/4 time there are three crotchets per bar. There is one **strong beat**, which is the first beat of the bar, followed by two weak beats.

The **quavers** can be beamed right across **two** or **three** whole crotchet beats, but the first note of the group must fall **on** the beat, not on an off beat.

All correct   Incorrect

In the above bars, all are correct except the last one. In the last bar, the 4th quaver falls on an off beat.

Groups with **semiquavers** are normally only beamed to make up **one** crotchet beat maximum.

Here are some examples:

BEAMING IN 4/4 TIME

In 4/4 time there are four crotchet beats per bar.

The first beat of the bar is the strong beat. The second and fourth beats are the weak beats. But the **third** beat is a **secondary strong beat**.

This means that the first beat of the bar has the strongest accent, the third beat has a slightly weaker accent, and the second and fourth beats receive no accent.

This is reflected in the beaming: you can beam together quavers which make up to **two crotchets'** worth of beats, but **only** if they fall on beats 1-2 or 3-4. You **cannot** beam together quavers or semiquavers which cross from beats 2-3.

Correct   Correct   Incorrect

Bar 1 is correct, because the first quaver in each group falls on a strong beat.

Bar 2 is correct, because the first quaver in the first group falls on a weak beat and the first of the second group on a stronger beat. This makes the secondary strong beat obvious.

Bar 3 is incorrect, because the 3rd quaver in the group should have a stronger accent than the first quaver. The importance of the third beat of the bar is hidden.

Groups which contain semiquavers should normally equal a maximum of one or two crotchets.

Here are some examples.

Notice that:

- The first four notes in bar 1 are all beamed together, making a group worth a minim.

- In bar 2, there is one unbeamed quaver. It can't be beamed to the next group because that group needs to start on the third beat of the bar, to show the place of the secondary strong beat.

- Bar 3 looks complicated, but it's not really! The first (strongest) beat is the first rest plus the beamed semiquaver and quaver. Together, they make up one crotchet's beat. The second (weak) beat is made up of three beamed semiquavers and a semiquaver's silence. The third (secondary strong beat) begins on the dotted quaver, and the final (weak) is the same as the second beat.

- In bar 3, it would be better not to beam the notes into groups worth a minim, because it will make it much more difficult to see which of the notes falls on the 2nd or 4th beat.

46

Stem Direction - Beaming Two Notes

If you need to join two or more notes together, but some of them have stems which point up and others which point down, which direction do you choose for the beamed group? For example, let's say you had to beam together two Ds of different pitches. Should they both have upwards pointing stems, or downwards pointing?

To work out which way to draw your stems when beaming two or more notes, first you need to work out which note is **furthest** from the middle line.

In our example above, the bottom D is further away from the middle line than the top D is.

Use the direction of the note which is furthest from the middle line as your guide.

The bottom D has its stem pointing upwards, so that's the direction we should use with our beaming:

However, if we change the notes to Fs, you will notice that we have to change to stems down, because the top F is further from the middle line than the bottom F, so in this case the beamed notes have their stems the other way round.

Angling Beams

Beams can be flat, angled up or angled down. Beaming should follow the general direction of the music, from left to right.

If the music is getting higher, the beam should point upwards; if it's getting lower it should be downwards. If the pitch of the beamed notes is the same overall, the beam should be flat.

Sometimes you may need to make the stems on some notes extra-long, to allow enough space for everything to be seen.

Bars 1-4 are correct.

In bar 4, the stems are extra-long on the lower Es, to allow space for the high E.

In bar 5, the beams is flat but the music is rising - this is bad practice.

In bar 6, the music is falling, but the beam is angled upwards, this is incorrect.

In bar 7, the pitch of the first and last notes is the same, so the beam should be flat.

8. BEAMING (USA)

Notes which are smaller than a quarter note - eighth notes and sixteenth notes - have tails attached to their stems.

To make music easier to read, we normally group these small notes together in **complete beats**. To do this, we join the tails together, making them into a straight line.

We call this line a "beam"- they are **beamed notes**.

MAKING BEAMED NOTES

Notes with one tail (eighth notes and dotted eighth notes) have one beam. Sixteenth notes have two tails so they have two beams, which are drawn quite close together.

Here are some examples of beamed eighth note notes.

Eighth notes can be beamed to sixteenth notes like this:

We can also join dotted eighth notes to sixteenth notes with beams, like this:

Notice that the lower sixteenth note beam is quite short. This is a cut-off beam.

Cut-off beams should be about as wide as the note-head. They can point in either direction, depending on which side of the eighth note they are on.

Here's another example of beamed notes which have cut-off beams:

Beaming and Beats

In the time signatures you need to know for Grade 1 Music Theory (2/4, 3/4 and 4/4), the **beat** is always represented by a **quarter note** time value.

(In other time signatures the beat could be an eighth note or half note. However, in this lesson we are assuming the beat is always a quarter note.)

In each measure, some notes are played a tiny bit louder than others - this slight accent is what gives music its feeling of pulse.

Beats are categorized as follows:

- **Strong beat**: this is the strongest accent in the measure and falls right at the beginning of the measure.

- **Weak beat**: these are the other quarter note beats of the measure.

- **Off beat**: these are any notes which fall in between the strong and/or weak beats.

The rules for correct beaming depend on the **time signature** in use.

You'll need to learn the rules for each time signature separately, as well as these general rules:

- The eighth notes and sixteenth notes should be joined together to make the quarter note beat obvious.

- Beams never cross over the bar lines.

- The first note of a beamed group must never fall **on an off beat**, unless it's preceded by a rest or a dotted note.

Beaming and Rests

We can include rests inside a group of beamed notes. Rests themselves are never beamed - we simply squeeze them between the notes.

We can change their vertical position on the stave if we need to, to make the music clearer.

The sixteenth rest has been moved downwards a little bit, so that it doesn't get mixed up with the beam lines.

Beaming in 2/4 Time

In 2/4 time there are two quarter note beats per measure. There is one **strong beat**, which is the first beat of the measure. The second quarter note beat is the weak beat.

Notes are normally beamed together to make up one quarter note beat. Here are some examples.

If there are four eighth notes in a measure, they can all be beamed together.

Both correct

Beaming in 3/4 Time

In 3/4 time there are three quarter notes per measure. There is one **strong beat**, which is the first beat of the measure, followed by two weak beats.

The **eighth notes** can be beamed right across **two** or **three** quarter note beats, but the first note of the group must fall **on** the beat, not on an off beat.

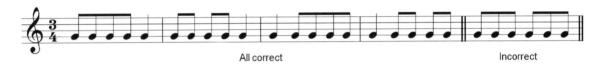

All correct   Incorrect

In the above measures, all are correct except the last one. In the last measure, the 4th eighth note falls on an off beat.

Groups with **sixteenth notes** are normally only beamed to make up **one** quarter note beat maximum.

Here are some examples:

Beaming in 4/4 Time

In 4/4 time there are four quarter note beats per measure.

The first beat of the measure is the strong beat. The second and fourth beats are the weak beats. But the **third** beat is a **secondary strong beat**.

This means that the first beat of the measure has the strongest accent, the third beat has a slightly weaker accent, and the second and fourth beats receive no accent.

This is reflected in the beaming: you can beam together eighth notes which make up to **two quarter notes'** worth of beats, but **only** if they fall on beats 1-2 or 3-4. You **cannot** beam together eighth notes or sixteenth notes which cross from beats 2-3.

Measure 1 is correct, because the first eighth note in each group falls on a strong beat.

Measure 2 is correct, because the first eighth note in the first group falls on a weak beat and the first of the second group on a stronger beat. This makes the secondary strong beat obvious.

Measure 3 is incorrect, because the 3rd eighth note in the group should have a stronger accent than the first eighth note. The importance of the third beat of the measure is hidden.

Groups which contain sixteenth notes should normally equal a maximum of one or two quarter notes.

Here are some examples.

Notice that:

- The first four notes in measure 1 are all beamed together, making a group worth a half note.

- In measure 2, there is one unbeamed eighth note. It can't be beamed to the next group because that group needs to start on the third beat of the measure, to show the place of the secondary strong beat.

- Measure 3 looks complicated, but it's not really! The first (strongest) beat is the first rest plus the beamed sixteenth note and eighth note. Together, they make up one quarter note's beat. The second (weak) beat is made up of three beamed sixteenth notes and a sixteenth note's silence. The third (secondary strong beat) begins on the dotted eighth note, and the final (weak) is the same as the second beat.

- In measure 3, it would be better not to beam the notes into groups worth a half note, because it will make it much more difficult to see which of the notes falls on the 2nd or 4th beat.

STEM DIRECTION - BEAMING TWO NOTES

If you need to join two or more notes together, but some of them have stems which point up and others which point down, which direction do you choose for the beamed group? For example, let's say you had to beam together two Ds of different pitches. Should they both have upwards pointing stems, or downwards pointing?

To work out which way to draw your stems when beaming two or more notes, first you need to work out which note is **furthest** from the middle line.

In our example above, the bottom D is further away from the middle line than the top D is.

Use the direction of the note which is furthest from the middle line as your guide.

The bottom D has its stem pointing upwards, so that's the direction we should use with our beaming:

However, if we change the notes to Fs, you will notice that we have to change to stems down, because the top F is further from the middle line than the bottom F, so in this case the beamed notes have their stems the other way round.

ANGLING BEAMS

Beams can be flat, angled up or angled down. Beaming should follow the general direction of the music, from left to right.

If the music is getting higher, the beam should point upwards; if it's getting lower it should be downwards. If the pitch of the beamed notes is the same overall, the beam should be flat.

Sometimes you may need to make the stems on some notes extra-long, to allow enough space for everything to be seen.

Measures 1-4 are correct.

In measure 4, the stems are extra-long on the lower Es, to allow space for the high E.

In measure 5, the beams is flat but the music is rising - this is incorrect.

In measure 6, the music is falling, but the beam is angled upwards, this is incorrect.

In measure 7, the pitch of the first and last notes is the same, so the beam should be flat.

8. BEAMING EXERCISES

EXERCISE 1

Copy the following melodies with correct beaming and stem direction.

a.

b.

c.

EXERCISE 2

The following melodies contain errors in beaming and stem direction. Write them out correctly.

a.

b.

8. BEAMING ANSWERS

a.

(Bar one would also be correct with all four notes beamed together.)

b.

Alternative answer:

c.

a.

(Bar 4 is also correct if written in three groups of two quavers (eighth notes).

b.

9. TIES

In music theory, a tie is a small, curved line which connects two notes of exactly the **same pitch**. The time values of tied notes are added together to make a longer note - you only play the note once.

Be careful not to confuse ties and slurs! A tie looks exactly like a slur - but a slur connects two notes of a **different pitch** and tells the player to play the two notes smoothly. The first example shows two tied Fs, the second example shows an F slurred to a G.

WHY TIES?

Ties are used for three reasons.

1. When a note has to be held **across a bar line**.

2. When the length of the note is difficult/impossible to express with a **single** note value. Here, the A is worth a count of 2 and a quarter beats.

3. To allow the **beat** to be clearly seen. In 4/4 for example, the third beat (which is the secondary strong beat) should be easy to spot. Bar 1 is correct - by tying two quavers (8th notes), we can see where the third beat starts. Bar 2 uses the same overall note values, but it is difficult to see at first glance where the second strong beat of the bar is.

POSITIONING TIES

Ties are usually written on the **opposite** side of a musical note to its stem. In the examples that we just looked at, the F's have their stems down, so the tie is placed above the notes. The As are stems up, so the tie is drawn below the notes.

TIES AND ACCIDENTALS

An accidental placed on the first of two tied notes also applies to the second tied note, even if the two notes are separated by a bar line. The first note in bar 2 is also a G sharp.

Sometimes you might see an accidental in brackets on the second note. This is called a "courtesy" accidental - it's only there to make it clear what the note is supposed to be.

TIES AND BEAMS

We don't normally combine ties and beams on the same notes: break the beam over two tied notes. Bar 1 is correct: the beam is broken so that the second tied note starts a new beamed group. Bar 2 is incorrect.

9. TIES EXERCISES

EXERCISE 1

a. What effect does a tie have?

b. How can you tell the difference between a tie and a slur?

c. When should a tie be written above a note, and when below?

EXERCISE 2

Tie together all the notes which it is possible to tie.

EXERCISE 3

Write ONE note which has the same time value as the tied notes. An example is given.

EXERCISE 4

Circle any ties which are incorrect.

EXERCISE 5

How long should you count each of these pairs of tied notes for?

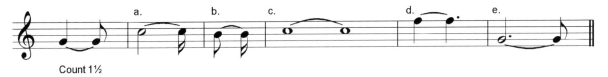

Count 1½

9. TIES ANSWERS

EXERCISE 1

a. It adds the time values of the two notes together.

b. Only notes of the same pitch can be tied. Notes of different pitches can only be slurred.

c. Ties are written above notes with downward pointing stems, and below notes with upward pointing stems.

EXERCISE 2

EXERCISE 3

EXERCISE 4

EXERCISE 5

a. 2¼   c. 8   e. 3½

b. ¾   d. 2½

10. TONES AND SEMITONES (HALF AND WHOLE STEPS)

SEMITONES (HALF STEPS)

A semitone (or "half step" in the USA) is the smallest distance between two different notes.

Let's use the piano keyboard to look at some examples of semitones.

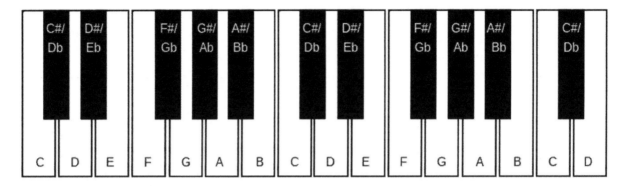

If two notes are as close as possible on the piano keyboard, the distance between them is a **semitone**.

Find E and F next to each other on the piano keyboard.

The distance between E and F is a semitone; it's not possible to squeeze another note in between them, because there is nothing between them on the piano keyboard.

Now find A and B flat. The distance between A and B flat is also a semitone.

TONES (WHOLE STEPS)

If there is **one** note between the two notes we are looking at, the distance between those two notes is called a tone. A tone is the same distance as two semitones.

Find G and A on the keyboard. G-A is a tone. We can squeeze a G sharp/A flat between them.

E-F sharp is another tone. F natural sits between them.

LIST OF SEMITONES (HALF STEPS)

Here is a list of the most common semitones:

C - C#/Db	C#/Db - D	D - D#/Eb	D#/Eb - E	E - F	F - F#/Gb
F#/Gb - G	G - G#/Ab	G#/Ab - A	A - A#/Bb	A#/Bb - B	B - C

LIST OF TONES (WHOLE STEPS)

C - D	C#/Db - D#-Eb	D - E	D#/Eb - F	E - F#/Gb	F - G
F#/Gb - G#/Ab	G - A	G#/Ab - A#/Bb	A - B	A#/Bb - C	B - C#/Db

If you find it confusing to remember where the semitones and tones are, it can be helpful to draw a little diagram of a piano keyboard to help you work it out.

To sketch a piano keyboard, start by drawing a rectangle and then divide it into eight smaller rectangles – these are the white notes on the piano keyboard. Label them from C to C.

Then draw black rectangles between the notes, in the following pattern: 2 – gap – 3

10. TONES AND SEMITONES EXERCISES

EXERCISE 1

Describe each of these pairs of notes as **semitones (half steps)** or **tones (whole steps)**.

EXERCISE 2

As exercise 1. This time the notes are in the bass clef.

EXERCISE 3

Write a **higher** note as indicated. An example is given.

EXERCISE 4

Write a **lower** note as indicated.

10. TONES AND SEMITONES ANSWERS

EXERCISE 1

a. Tone (whole step)
b. Semitone (half step)
c. Tone
d. Tone
e. Semitone
f. Semitone
g. Semitone
h. Tone
i. Semitone

EXERCISE 2

a. Semitone
b. Semitone
c. Tone
d. Tone
e. Tone
f. Semitone
g. Semitone
h. Semitone
i. Tone

EXERCISE 3

EXERCISE 4

11. MAJOR SCALES & SCALE DEGREES

A "scale" is **any** series of musical notes which is defined by its pattern of tones and semitones.

THE C MAJOR SCALE

Play or sing this series of eight notes:

This is a scale of **C major**. In the C major scale, both the first and the last notes are Cs- but how do we know what the in-between notes are?

On the piano, a C major scale uses all the **white** notes (so it doesn't have any sharps or flats), but on other instruments, we don't have "white" notes, so how do we know which notes to use?

In fact, what we need to know is the **distance** between each of the notes in the scale. The distance between any two notes of the scale which are next to each other will be either a **tone** or a **semitone**.

All major scales are built from same pattern of tones and semitones.

TONES AND SEMITONES IN THE MAJOR SCALE

Let's look at the C major scale again, and see what the pattern of tones and semitones is.

The distance between each pair of notes is written below the stave: T for tones (whole steps) and S for semitones (half steps):

The pattern in the ascending (rising) C major scale is T-T-S-T-T-T-S.

All ascending major scales follow the same pattern of tones and semitones, so try to remember it! The same pattern is used, whether the scale is written in the treble or bass clef.

T – T – S – T – T – T – S

On the way down, the scale is reversed. This means the pattern of tones and semitones is also reversed. The pattern for a descending major scale is:

S – T – T – T – S – T – T

G, D and F Major Scales

In ABRSM Grade One music theory, you need to know about four major scales: C, G, D and F major.

Here's a picture of the piano keyboard, to help you remember the layout of notes:

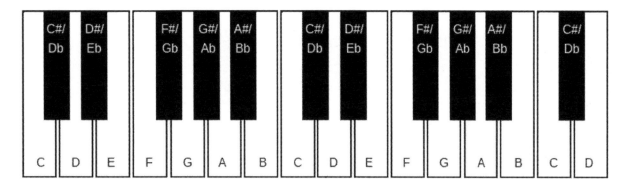

G Major Scale

Let's look at G major next. We'll construct the scale using the T-T-S-T-T-T-S pattern that we've just learnt.

We'll start by putting the first G on the stave. We're using the treble clef, but it works just the same way in the bass clef.

The next note we need, as you can see from the pattern above, is a tone higher than G. The note which is a tone higher than G is **A**, (because we can squeeze a G sharp/A flat between them). So A is our next note:

The third note is, again, a tone up. From A, the next tone up is B, (we can squeeze A sharp/B flat in between them).

Next we meet our first semitone - C. (There is nothing we can squeeze in between B and C).

Hopefully by now you've got the idea, so here are the rest of the notes of the G major scale:

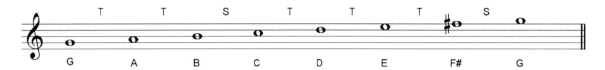

G major has one sharp - F sharp. You might be wondering why we choose F sharp and not G flat, since they are the same note on the piano.

When we write a scale, we use **each letter of the alphabet once only**, except for the first and last notes which must have the same letter.

G major must start and end on **G**, so we've already used up that letter. We haven't used F though, so we need to use that, and make it into F sharp.

D MAJOR SCALE

Let's look at D major next:

The scale of D major has two sharps - F sharp and C sharp. These make the semitone steps in the scale, from F#-G and from C#-D.

F MAJOR SCALE

The last scale we need to look at for the grade one music theory exam is F major:

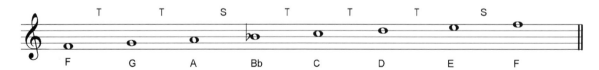

The F major scale doesn't have any sharps, but it has one flat - B flat. This makes the first semitone step in the scale, from A to Bb.

Remember, we can't use A sharp instead of B flat, because we've already got an A in the scale.

WRITING DESCENDING SCALES

Scales can be written going up or going down.

Scales which go up are called "ascending", and scales which go down are "descending".

When we write a descending scale, the pattern of tones and semitones is reversed, so instead of being T-T-S-T-T-T-S, it is S-T-T-T-S-T-T.

Here's the F major descending scale.

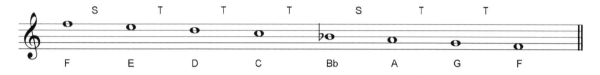

You don't need to remember the order of tones and semitones back-to-front, just write the scales **backwards**, starting on the right side of the stave instead of the left.

DEGREES OF THE SCALE

The first and last notes in any scale are called the "tonic" or "keynote".

The other notes can be referred to by **number**.

For example, in C major, the second note in the scale is D, so we can say that D is the **2nd degree of the scale of C major**.

We always use the **ascending** scale to work out the degrees of a scale.

Every scale has seven degrees, because there are seven different notes.

The last note of the scale is another tonic note.

Here's a summary of the degrees of the scales of C, D, G and F major:

	Tonic (1st)	2nd	3rd	4th	5th	6th	7th	Tonic
C Major	C	D	E	F	G	A	B	C
G Major	G	A	B	C	D	E	F#	G
D Major	D	E	F#	G	A	B	C#	D
F Major	F	G	A	Bb	C	D	E	F

11. MAJOR SCALES & SCALE DEGREES EXERCISES

EXERCISE 1

a.   How many semitone steps are there in one octave of a major scale?

b.   What's the pattern of tones (whole steps) and semitones (half steps) in ascending major scales?

EXERCISE 2

Name the degree of the scale (e.g. 2nd, 3rd, 4th) of the notes marked *.

a. The key is F major

b. The key is G major

EXERCISE 3

Write as semibreves (whole notes) the scales named below. Add any necessary sharp or flat signs.

a. C major descending

b. D major ascending

EXERCISE 4

Name the key of each of these scales. Draw a bracket over each pair of notes making a semitone.

EXERCISE 5

This melody uses all the notes of the scale of C major - true or false?

11. MAJOR SCALES AND SCALE DEGREES ANSWERS

EXERCISE 1

a. Two.

b. T − T − S − T − T − T − S

EXERCISE 2

a.

b.

EXERCISE 3

a.

b.

EXERCISE 4

a.

b.

EXERCISE 4

False. The melody doesn't contain an A.

12. KEY SIGNATURES

KEY

When we write music which mostly uses notes from the scale of C major and sounds good finished with a C, we say that the music is "in the key of C major" or "in C a major".

Here's a short tune in C major:

G MAJOR KEY SIGNATURE

If a tune mostly uses the notes from the G major scale and sounds good finished with a G, then the music is "in G major".

The scale of G major contains the notes G-A-B-C-D-E-F#. The key of G major contains F sharps, not F naturals.

Instead of writing all the Fs in the piece with sharp signs next to them, we write just one F sharp, right at the beginning of the staff, after the clef and before the time signature.

This is called the "**key signature**".

In the treble clef, we always write the F sharp sign on the top line (we never use the lower F space). You should be able to just see the line of the stave between the two horizontal lines of the sharp sign.

In the bass clef, we write the sign for F sharp on the second line from the top.

The key signature is written at the beginning of every staff of music, immediately after the clef, to remind us that all the Fs need to be F sharps. (We don't use a key signature for music which is in C major, because we don't need one! - C major doesn't have any sharps or flats!)

The key signature is there to remind us that all the F's in the piece should be F#s. It applies to ALL the pitches of F, not just the one on the top/2nd line of the stave.

Here's the same tune as above, but now it's in G major:

D Major Key Signature

Let's look at D major next:

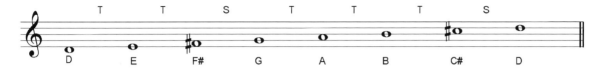

The scale of D major has two sharps - F sharp and C sharp. This means that music written in the key of D major has F#s and C#s too.

The key signature of D major in the treble clef looks like this:

We add the C sharp after the F sharp that we've got already.

In the bass clef, the key signature of D major looks like this.

F major Key Signature

Finally, let's look at the key signature for F major. Remember that in F major there aren't any sharps, but there is one flat - B flat.

In the treble clef, the flat is written on the middle line.

In the bass clef, the flat is written on the second line from the bottom.

For Grade One Music Theory, you only need to know about these three key signatures: G major, D major and F major (and you need to know that C major doesn't need one!)

Make sure you know which order to write the sharps in the key signature for D major, and make sure that each sharp/flat in a key signature is positioned on the right line/space.

12. KEY SIGNATURES EXERCISES

EXERCISE 1

Name the major keys shown by these key signatures.

a.

c.

b.

d.

EXERCISE 2

Add the correct key signatures to these bars.

a. D major

b. F major

C. G major

EXERCISE 3

Give the letter name of each of the notes marked *, including the sharp or flat sign where necessary.

12 KEY SIGNATURES ANSWERS

EXERCISE 1

Name the major keys shown by these key signatures.

- a. F major
- b. G major
- c. D major
- d. F major

EXERCISE 2

a.

EXERCISE 3

13. INTERVALS

An interval is the distance between two notes, measured as a **number**. In Grade One Music Theory, sometimes you have to measure given intervals, and sometimes you have to write notes at a certain interval.

MELODIC AND HARMONIC INTERVALS

We can measure the distance between two notes which are played **together** at the same time, like these:

The distance between these notes is called a "harmonic" interval.

Or we can measure two notes which are played separately, like these:

The distance between these notes is called a "melodic" interval.

We use the **same** method to measure both kinds of interval.

MEASURING INTERVALS

When we measure an interval, we always start counting from the **lower** note.

We then count upwards to the higher note.

Here, we start counting on the lower note, which is C. We count upwards to the higher note, E. This gives us C, D and E. We counted three letter names, so this interval is called a **third**.

If we count four letter names, the interval is a **fourth**, and so on, until we reach a **seventh**.

If we count eight notes and arrive back at the same letter, the interval is called an "**octave**".

If the two notes are the same pitch, it's called a "**unison**".

In Grade One Music Theory, all the intervals you have to calculate will start on the tonic (1st note) of the scale. Here are the intervals built from a tonic C:

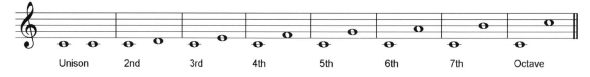

| Unison | 2nd | 3rd | 4th | 5th | 6th | 7th | Octave |

INTERVALS IN DIFFERENT KEYS

In Grade One Music Theory, you need to know about intervals in C major, G major, D major and F major.

The method for working out intervals is always the same, no matter what the key is. However, don't forget that in G major you need F sharp, in D major you need F sharp and C sharp, and in F major you need B flat.

For example, in D major, a harmonic interval of a third will be this:

We start counting on the lower note, D. We count D, E and F sharp - three letter names, so the interval is a third.

In F major, an interval of a fourth will have a B flat:

We count F, G, A and B flat - four letter names, so it's a fourth.

WRITING INTERVALS

When you write intervals in your music theory exam, first you need to work out which notes you have to write, and secondly you need to write the notes clearly and accurately.

If you have to write an interval, you will be given the first (lower) note of the two, and you will be told what interval to calculate; something like this:

You'll also be told if you have to write a **harmonic**, or **melodic** interval. This one is a melodic interval, so we'll write the second note **after** the given note.

Remember that we start counting on the **lower** note, which is F in our example. We've been told to write a **7th**, so we count **7** letter names upwards (including the first letter): F, G, A, B flat, C, D, E.

The seventh note is E, so that's the note we need to write.

Don't forget that we were told to write a **melodic** interval, so in this case we will write the E after the F, and not directly above it:

Don't forget to look carefully at the **clefs** - you will normally have about 3 questions with the treble clef, and 3 with the bass.

Some intervals are a bit more awkward to write. They are the harmonic unison and 2nd.

Harmonic intervals are written directly **above** the given note, but the unison is the same note, and the 2nd is too close to write directly above. We have to move these notes to the **side** a little.

If you try to write a 2nd directly above, you will produce something unreadable like this:

13. INTERVALS EXERCISES

EXERCISE 1

Give the number (e.g. 2nd, 3rd, 4th etc.) of each of these melodic intervals.

EXERCISE 2

Above each note, write a higher note to make the named **harmonic interval**. The key is C major.

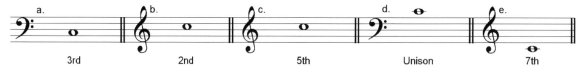

EXERCISE 3

Above each note, write a higher note to make the named **harmonic interval**. The key is F major.

EXERCISE 4

Next to each note, write a higher note to make the named **melodic interval**. The key is D major.

EXERCISE 5

Next to each note, write a higher note to make the named **melodic interval**. The key is G major.

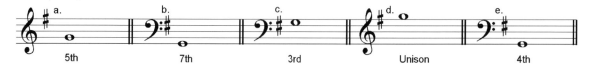

EXERCISE 6

Next to each note, write another note to make the named **melodic interval**. Include any necessary accidentals. The key is given in each case.

13. INTERVALS ANSWERS

EXERCISE 1

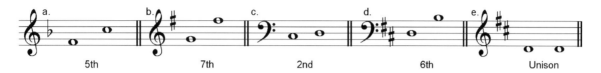

EXERCISE 2

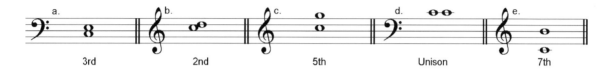

EXERCISE 3

EXERCISE 4

EXERCISE 5

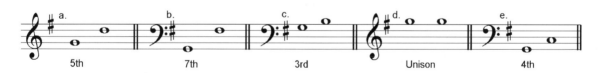

EXERCISE 6

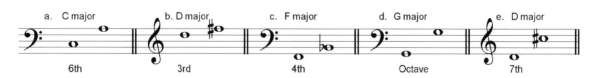

14. TONIC TRIADS

The **tonic** is the first (and last) note in a scale. "**Triad**" means "chord built with thirds".

A "tonic triad" is a music theory term for a chord of **three notes** and the lowest of these notes is the **tonic** (keynote) of the key we are in.

Here's a tonic triad in G major:

BUILDING TONIC TRIADS

Tonic triads are simple to build. You don't need to build them yourself in Grade One music theory, but it's pretty easy so I'll show you how anyway!

First you need to know what key you are in. Remember that for Grade One music theory, you only need to know the keys of C major, G major, D major and F major.

Let's build a D major tonic triad.

The tonic is the first note of the scale. We are in D major, so D is the tonic. That's the first note we need to write down. It's going to be the lowest note of the chord, so we'll write a low D, so that we have room to add notes above it:

The next note in the triad is the third note of the scale. The third note in the scale is F sharp, so we'll add that one now:

The last note of the chord is the fifth note of the scale, which for our triad is A:

Here is our finished tonic triad in the key of D major!

Tonic triads are always made up of the tonic, third and fifth notes of the scale.

We say that tonic triads are built out of **thirds**, because the interval between the lowest note and the middle note is a third, and the interval between the middle note and the highest note is also a third.

76

NAMING THE KEY OF TONIC TRIADS

In Grade One Music Theory, you might be asked to name the key of some tonic triads. This is very easy to do if you remember that the lowest note in the chord will give you the answer. For example, if the lowest note is C, then the key will be C major.

You only need to know about major keys for Grade One Music Theory, so you won't have to identify any minor keys (in any part of the exam).

So, you have four possible answers: C major, D major, G major or F major.

Make sure you pay attention to the clef.

Here's an example question.

Name the key of this tonic triad:

The lowest note is F, so it's an F major tonic triad.

ADDING CLEFS AND KEY SIGNATURES

In the exam, you might be asked to add a clef and key signature to some tonic triads. You will be told the key of the triads. Here's an example:

G major

Add the correct clef and key signature to this tonic triad.

Look at the lowest note of the triad, and think about what that note would be with a treble clef, and with a bass clef. In our example, if we had a treble clef, the lowest note would be E. If we had a bass clef, it would be G. We need a G, so it must be bass clef.

G major

Here's the clef added. Make sure you draw your clefs carefully. Look at Lesson 19 - Handwriting Music for more on drawing clefs.

Next we need to add the correct key signature for G major in the bass clef:

G major

Look at Lesson 12 - Key Signatures if you need help on how to write key signatures.

14. TONIC TRIADS EXERCISES

EXERCISE 1

1. How many different notes are there in a tonic triad?

2. Which note of a tonic triad is the tonic of the scale – the lowest, middle or highest?

3. Which four key signatures do you need to know for the Grade 1 music theory exam?

EXERCISE 2

Name the keys of each of these tonic triads, e.g. "C major".

EXERCISE 3

Add the necessary **clef** and **key signature** to make the named tonic triads.

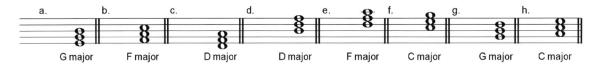

G major   F major   D major   D major   F major   C major   G major   C major

EXERCISE 4

1. Which bar contains all the notes which make up the tonic triad in G major?

2. Which bar contains all the notes which make up the tonic triad in D major?

14. TONIC TRIADS ANSWERS

EXERCISE 1

1. Three.

2. The lowest.

3. C major, G major, D major and F major.

EXERCISE 2

EXERCISE 3

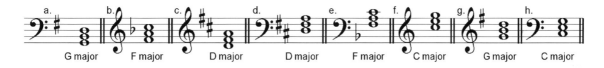

EXERCISE 4

1. Bar 5 (G, B and D)

2. Bar 2 (D, F# and A)

15. DYNAMICS

DYNAMICS - OR "VOLUME CONTROL"

"Dynamics" are all about the volume of music - is it quiet or loud, does it increase or decrease in volume?

STATIC OR CHANGING?

Players need to understand quite a few different words (and abbreviations or "short forms") for dynamics. To make things easier, we can group these words/abbreviations into two categories - **static and changing.**

- A **static** dynamic means that the **all** the music should be played at that volume, until another direction is given.

- A **changing** dynamic means that the music should **gradually** begin to change in volume (up or down) and continue changing until the next direction.

STATIC DYNAMICS

We use Italian words or abbreviations to indicate static dynamics.
Piano means "quietly" or "softly", and **forte** means "loudly". *Piano* is shortened to **p** and *forte* is shortened to **f**.

Mezzo means "half" (or "in-between"), and it is shortened to **m**. Usually we translate this as "moderately" for dynamics.

The ending **-issimo** on a word means "very"- it's indicated by a double *p* or a double *f*.
This gives us six possibilities: here they are in order from loudest to quietest:

ff	= Fortissimo	= very loud	*mp*	= Mezzo Piano	= moderately quiet
f	= Forte	= loud	*p*	= Piano	= quiet
mf	= Mezzo Forte	= moderately loud	*pp*	= Pianissimo	= very quiet

CHANGING DYNAMICS

Gradual increases in volume are shown either with Italian words, or with symbols.
Crescendo (pronounced "kre-<u>shen</u>-do") means "gradually getting louder", and is shortened to *cresc.*

Diminuendo (pronounced "di-min-yu-<u>en</u>-do") means "gradually getting quieter", and is shortened to *dim. Decrescendo* means the same thing.

The same instructions can be given with "hairpin" symbols:

getting louder   getting quieter

The hairpin is placed under the first and last notes of the section with changing dynamics.

15. DYNAMICS EXERCISES

EXERCISE 1

Write out the dynamics *p - mf - ff - pp - f - mp* in the correct order, from the loudest to the quietest. The first answer is given.

ff -

EXERCISE 2

Explain the following in English:

a.

b.
c.   *Mezzo forte*
d.   *Pianissimo*

EXERCISE 3

Draw a circle around the note in this melody which would sound the loudest.

81

15. DYNAMICS ANSWERS

EXERCISE 1

ff – f – mf – mp – p – pp

EXERCISE 2

    a.   Gradually getting louder

    b.   Gradually getting quieter/softer

    c.   Moderately loud

    d.   Very quiet/soft

EXERCISE 3

16. SYMBOLS

Symbols in music have many different shapes and uses. They are useful because they give us information quickly, without us having to read words.

Symbols which are attached to notes are normally written on the opposite side to the stem.

These are the symbols you need to know for Grade One Music Theory. Make sure you know how to explain each one in words! If the symbol has a foreign name, such as "staccato", you need to know how to explain it **in English** in the exam, for full marks.

Tie
The two (or more) notes should be played as one note.

Slur (or "Legato")
The two (or more) notes should be played smoothly.

The Accent

Accent. Attack the note with a hard force.

The Crescendo and Decrescendo
Crescendo. Gradually getting louder.

Decrescendo or Diminuendo. Gradually getting quieter.

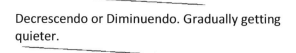

Staccato
Staccato. Play the note short and detached.

Pause (or Fermata)
Hold on to the note for some time longer than real value of the note.

Repeat
Single repeat bar. Go back to the beginning and repeat everything up to this bar.

Double repeat bars.
Repeat everything between the two repeat bars.

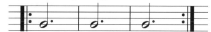

16. SYMBOLS EXERCISES

What do these symbols mean? Explain using English words.

a.

b.

c.

d.

e.

f.

g.

h.

i.

16. SYMBOLS ANSWERS

    a.   Repeat from the beginning

    b.   Short and detached

    c.   Pause on the note

    d.   Gradually getting quieter

    e.   Slur – play the notes smoothly

    f.   Accent – attack the note with force

    g.   Tie – add the note values together

    h.   Repeat the bars between the double dots

    i.   Gradually getting louder

17. ITALIAN TERMS

In Grade One Music Theory, you need to know what a handful of Italian terms mean in music.

People often wonder why most musical terms are in Italian and not another language, but actually lots of other languages have been used by composers, in particular German and French.

Italy was the birthplace of the Renaissance Era (from about 1350 onwards), and was the place where classical music really took off a few centuries later. Composers from many countries used Italian terms because they were associated with musical excellence, and were understood around the world. Today people think of Italian terms as the normal language in music.

From the Grade 4 music theory exam onwards you'll need to know foreign terms not only in Italian, but also in French and German!

LIST OF TERMS

Here is a complete list of all the Italian terms for Grade One Music Theory.

It's easier to learn foreign terms if you learn them in groups, and only try to learn a few each day.

The strongest syllable is in *italics*.

ITALIAN TERM	PRONUNCIATION	ABBREVIATION	ENGLISH MEANING
TEMPO			
A tempo	a *tem*poh		At the original speed /time
Accelerando	a-che-le-*ran*-doh	Accel.	Gradually getting faster
Adagio	a-*dah*-jioh		Slowly
Allegretto	a-le-*gre*-toh		Fairly quick
Allegro moderato	a-*le*-groh mo-de-*ra*-toh		Moderately quick
Andante	an-*dan*-te		At a walking pace
Lento	*len*-toh		Slow
Rallentando	ra-len-*tan*-doh	Rall.	Gradually getting slower
Ritardando	ri-tar-*dan*-doh	Rit.	Gradually getting slower
Ritenuto	ri-ten-*oo*-toh	Rit., Riten.	Held back

DYNAMICS			
Crescendo	cre-*shen*-doh	Cresc.	Gradually getting louder
Decrescendo	dee-cre-*shen*-doh	Decresc.	Gradually getting quieter
Diminuendo	di-mi-nyu-*en*-doh	Dim.	Gradually getting quieter
Forte	*for*-tay	F	Loud
Fortissimo	for-*tis*-i-moh	FF	Very loud
Mezzo forte	*met*-zoh *for*-tay	MF	Moderately loud
Mezzo piano	*met*-zoh *pya*-noh	MP	Moderately quiet
Pianissimo	pya-*ni*-si-moh	PP	Very quiet
Piano	*pyah*-noh	P	Quiet

PHRASING			
Cantabile	kan-*tar*-bi-lay		In a singing style
Legato	li-*ga*-toh		Smoothly
Staccato	sta-*kar*-toh		Short and detached

OTHER TERMS			
Da capo	da *ka*-poh	DC	From the beginning
Dal segno	dal *sen*-yoh	DS	𝄋 From the sign
Fine	*fee*-nay		The end
Mezzo	*met*-zo	M	Half
Moderato	mo-dur-*ar*-toh		Moderately
Poco	*poh*-koh	Poc.	A little

17. ITALIAN TERMS EXERCISES
GRADE 1 FOREIGN MUSICAL TERMS TEST

Give the English meaning of these musical terms.

1.	A tempo	15.	Fortissimo
2.	Cantabile	16.	Ritenuto
3.	Lento	17.	Mezzo piano
4.	Dal segno	18.	Piano
5.	Allegro moderato	19.	Fine
6.	Mezzo forte	20.	Legato
7.	Poco	21.	Ritardando
8.	Rallentando	22.	Da capo
9.	Forte	23.	Accelerando
10.	Staccato	24.	Crescendo
11.	Allegretto	25.	Diminuendo
12.	Decrescendo	26.	Moderato
13.	Mezzo	27.	Adagio
14.	Andante		

17. ITALIAN TERMS ANSWERS

1. In time
2. In a singing style
3. Slowly
4. From the sign
5. Moderately fast
6. Moderately loud
7. A little
8. Gradually slowing down
9. Loud
10. Short and detached
11. Fairly quick
12. Gradually getting softer
13. Moderate or half
14. At a walking pace
15. Very loud
16. Held back
17. Moderately soft
18. Soft/quiet
19. The end
20. Smoothly
21. Gradually slowing down
22. From the beginning
23. Gradually getting faster
24. Gradually getting louder
25. Gradually getting softer
26. Moderately
27. Slowly

18. HANDWRITING MUSIC

CLEARLY AND NEATLY

In the Grade One Music Theory exam, you need to be able to write music clearly and neatly. You will lose marks on any answer that the examiner finds difficult to read, has mistakes or is messy.

Every answer that you write has to be clear and neat, of course, but you will also have one question where you simply have to copy out about four bars of music. This question is worth ten points.

THREE TOOLS

You will need: pencils (take plenty of spares to your music theory exam!), an eraser and a ruler. Always write your answers in pencil. Make sure you've chosen a pencil which rubs out easily!

CLEFS, KEY SIGNATURES AND TIME SIGNATURES

 The treble clef should curl around the G line.

 The bass clef begins on the F line. The two dots are placed on either side of the F line.

 The order of sharps in key signatures is always F sharp then C sharp. Don't make sharp or flat signs too small or too big.

 The top number of the time signature fills the top half of the stave, the bottom number fills the bottom half.

Remember the order is always Clef - Key Signature - Time Signature (C-K-T).

WRITING NOTES AND BAR LINES

 Note heads are not perfectly round - they are egg-shaped and tilt upwards slightly.

Here's an extra-large crotchet (quarter note) to make it clear!

Use your ruler to draw note stems. Make the stems the same length - about 1cm is fine.

Notes above the middle of the stave usually have stems down, notes below the middle have stems up. Notes on the middle line should follow the general direction of the music.

To draw beamed notes neatly, first draw the stems of the first and last notes in the group. You will sometimes need to draw them a bit longer than normal.

Then draw the top horizontal beam.

Then fill in any other stems or beams as needed.

The first note in each bar should be about one note-head's width away from the bar line on its left. The other notes in a bar should be placed at relative distances.

This means that semiquavers (sixteenth notes) will be very close together, and semibreves (whole notes) will have a lot of space to the right of them.

This is correct: there is a larger space after the minim (half note), and smaller spaces after the smaller note values.

This is incorrect. The gap between the semiquavers (16th notes) is wider than the gap between the longer notes.

Ledger lines (the small lines on notes like middle C) should be the same distance as the other lines of the staff, and should not stick out too much to the left or right.

Make sure you use the correct note value when you write scales. Usually you will be told to use semibreves (whole notes).

Always draw barlines with a ruler. Make sure they don't stick out beyond the top or bottom lines of the stave.

Rests should be placed in the centre of the stave. Be very careful about the position of the minim (half) and semibreve (whole) rests.

COPYING MUSIC OUT EXACTLY

When you copy out music in your music theory exam, make sure you have copied absolutely every detail from the original.

Don't forget the dynamics, symbols like staccato or accents, any repeat bars, slurs, ties or bar numbers.

Use your ruler to make the distance between your notes as close as possible to the original. It's a good idea to draw the barlines in first, to make sure you don't run out of space.

Read the question carefully - don't copy out the wrong bars!

18. HANDWRITING MUSIC EXERCISES

This part of the music theory exam is something which is really easy to practise at home! Find any piece of music, take a piece of manuscript paper, and copy **exactly** what you see.

Choose music which has a lot of performance directions on it - dynamics, foreign terms and symbols, and choose music which has different rhythms, especially with beamed notes.

Use a well-sharpened pencil and a ruler.

When you've finished, look very carefully at your work for mistakes, or better still, ask somebody else to look at it for you (preferably someone who knows about music theory!)

Keep practising!

Here are a couple of excerpts you can try to copy:

GRADE 1 MUSIC THEORY - PRACTICE TEST: 1 HOUR

QUESTION 1

Add the time signature to each of these tunes. (6 points).

a.

b.

c.

QUESTION 2

Write the correct clef for each of these tonic triads. (4 points).

a. G major

b. F major

QUESTION 3

Copy out this melody, beaming the notes together correctly. (10 points).

QUESTION 4

Give the number (e.g. 2nd, 3rd, 4th) of each of these harmonic intervals, as shown in the first answer. (10 points).

QUESTION 5

Write the dynamics in the correct order, from the loudest to the quietest. The first answer is given. (10 points).

QUESTION 6

Next to each note write a rest that has the same time value, as shown in the first answer. (10 points)

QUESTION 7

Name the degree of the scale (e.g. 2nd, 3rd, 4th) of the notes marked *, as shown in the first answer. The key is C major. (8 points).

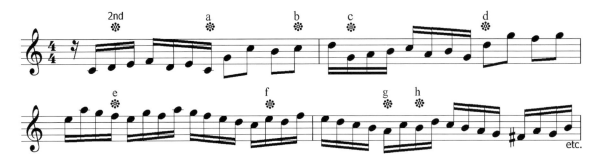

94

QUESTION 8

Circle two notes **next to each other** that are an interval of a 4th apart. (2 points).

QUESTION 9

Give the letter name of each of the notes marked a-h, including the sharp or flat sign where necessary. (8 points)

QUESTION 10

Write the named key signatures for each clef. An example is given. (10 points).

QUESTION 11

Look at this melody and then answer the questions below. (2 points per question).

a.   Give the time name (e.g. crotchet or quarter-note) of the rest in the first bar.

b.   *"Allegro moderato"* means 1) mostly fast, 2) very slow, 3) moderately quick or 4) fast and smooth?

c.   What does this curved line in bar 1 mean?

d.   What do these dots mean in bar 1?

e.   What does this symbol in bar 5 mean?

f.   What does the lower "4" in this time signature mean?

g.   Give the number of the bar which contains a crotchet (quarter note) rest.

h.   Give the letter name of the highest note.

i.   True or False? Bar 4 uses all the notes of the scale of G major.

j.   How many times does this rhythm occur?

k.   The key is G major. On which degree of the scale (e.g. 4th, 5th, 6th etc.) does the melody begin?

PRACTICE TEST ANSWERS

The test is scored out of 100.

- 66 points is needed for a pass.
- 80+ points = merit.
- 90+ points = distinction.

QUESTION 1

a. 2/4   b. 4/4   c. 3/4

QUESTION 2

QUESTION 3

QUESTION 4

a. Octave   c. 5th   e. 3rd

b. 6th   d. 2nd

QUESTION 5

QUESTION 6

QUESTION 7

a. 1st   d. 2nd   g. 6th

b. 1st   e. 4th   h. 7th

c. 5th   f. 3rd

QUESTION 8

mp

QUESTION 9

QUESTION 10

QUESTION 11

a.   Semiquaver (sixteenth note).

b.   (3) Moderately quick.

c.   Slur – play the notes smoothly.

d.   Staccato – short and detached.

e.   Pause – hold onto the note for longer than its normal time value.

f.   Count crotchet (quarter note) beats.

g.   Bar 5.

h.   G.

i.   True.

j.   Three times.

k.   5th.

ANNEX

RHYTHM

Prior to 2018, in the Grade One Music Theory exam, you had to write two bars of **rhythm** as an answer to two given bars. This question has been removed from the current ABRSM syllabus, but we include the lessons here for your reference. Learning how to compose is enjoyable and useful, and is still tested from grade 6 onwards, so we hope you will take the time to read through this reference section.

Write a two-bar rhythm as an answer to the given rhythm.

CHECK THE TIME SIGNATURE

The first thing you need to do is look at the time signature. This tells you **how many beats** you will need to write in each bar, so it's very important.

In the above question, the time signature is 2/4, so we will need to write note values which add up to two crotchet (quarter note) beats in each bar. Always double-check your finished rhythm to make sure you have the right number of beats.

When you beam (join) notes together, make sure that you beam each group correctly. See lesson "Lesson 8 Beaming" for more details about this.

LOOK AT THE EXISTING RHYTHMS

The next thing you should do is look at the kinds of rhythm which have **already** been used in the first two bars. What note values were used, and which values weren't used?

In our question, we've got crotchets (quarter notes), quavers (eighth notes) and semiquavers (sixteenth notes). We don't have any dotted notes, and we don't have any ties. You should use **similar** kinds of rhythms in your answering phrase as you have in the given phrase - each bar must have a connection.

RE-USE RHYTHMS

To write an answering rhythm, you should re-use some parts of the given rhythm, but don't just copy it exactly, of course!

Look at the "blocks" of rhythm which occur on each beat. We could describe the above rhythm as three different blocks like this:

1. crotchet (quarter note)

2. two quavers (eighth notes)

3. four semiquavers (sixteenth notes).

You could use the same blocks of rhythm but change their order. Make sure that no two bars are identical though!

Or you could keep a couple of the simpler blocks the same, but swap the others. You will get a maximum 7/10 for simply reversing the rhythm like this:

Or, you can even invent something completely new, but only for one or two beats' worth. For 10/10, you need to "reference the given material", which means reuse a bit of it, and then create something else which is new and interesting. This makes a balanced rhythm.

But watch out! It's not a good idea to invent completely new rhythms for the whole of the answering phrase - you are being marked on your sense of balance, not on how wildly creative you can be! Also, don't use too many rests. The examiner wants to see a rhythm, not bars of silence!

FINISHING CORRECTLY

You should end your phrase with a reasonably long note. Usually this means a **crotchet (quarter note)** or a **minim (half note)**. Phrases which end on quavers (eighth notes) or semiquavers (sixteenth notes) often sound too abrupt.

SAMPLE ANSWERS

Here are some example answers, with comments:

Comment: The semiquavers (16th notes) from the original have been reused, with some other imaginative material (e.g. the dotted rhythm). (10/10)

Comment: There is hardly any connection between the given and the answering phrase. There's no good reason for the rest at the end either. (8/10)

Comment: This is just an exact copy of the given bars. (7/10)

Comment: The number of beats in the third bar is wrong, bar 4 is a copy of bar 2. (5/10)

Comment: Nothing much of the given phrase has been used, both bars (3 &4) contain the wrong number of beats, and it's not a good idea to write exactly the same rhythm in each bar. (4/10)

RHYTHM EXERCISES
EXERCISE 1

In each of the following rhythms the answering phrase (bars 3 & 4) is not very good, but why? Explain **two faults** for each rhythm.

EXERCISE 2

Choose the best 2-bar answer (a-d) to the given rhythm. Explain your choice.

Choose your answer from rhythms a-d below.

RHYTHM ANSWERS

EXERCISE 1

a. The last bar has the wrong number of beats. It should end on a longer note value.

b. Bars 3 & 4 are exact copies of 2 & 1. It should end on a longer note value.

c. Bars 3 & 4 have nothing in common with bars 1 & 2. There is no reason for bar 4 to have two tied notes: a semibreve (whole note) is correct.

d. The notes in bar 3 are beamed incorrectly for 3/4 time (but correctly for 6/8 time). Bar 4 over-uses rests.

EXERCISE 2

a. Incorrect. Bars 3-4 have nothing in common with bars 1-2.

b. Incorrect. Bars 3-4 are simply bars 1-2 in reverse. The last note is too short.

c. Correct! Bars 3-4 re-use the dotted rhythm from the given opening and also contain some new material.

d. Incorrect. Bar 3 has the wrong number of beats (4.5)

Printed in Great Britain
by Amazon